POWERFUL POETICS

POETICS

for

Prayer

by

C h r i s t i n a   M a r i e   W o o d

AuthorHouse™
1663 Liberty Drive
Bloomington, IN 47403
www.authorhouse.com
Phone: 833-262-8899

Because of the dynamic nature of the Internet, any web addresses or links contained in this book may have changed since publication and may no longer be valid. The views expressed in this work are solely those of the author and do not necessarily reflect the views of the publisher, and the publisher hereby disclaims any responsibility for them.

Any people depicted in stock imagery provided by Getty Images are models, and such images are being used for illustrative purposes only.
Certain stock imagery © Getty Images.

This book is printed on acid-free paper.

ISBN: 979-8-8230-3698-6 (sc)
ISBN: 979-8-8230-3699-3 (e)
ISBN: 979-8-8230-3743-3 (hc)

Library of Congress Control Number: 2024923361

Print information available on the last page.

Published by AuthorHouse 12/17/2024

authorHOUSE®

Special Acknowledgements

I would like to thank my mother for being the first person to pray many of these poems with me.

The poem "Gifts from Heaven" was inspired by a prophecy from Alwyn Uys.

The poem "The Thousand Blessing" was inspired by teachings from Katie Souza.

The poem "Daughters of the Dawn" was written at Bonnie Jone's conference called "Daughters of the Dawn."

Special Tribute

My father, Daniel Wood lll, passed away on 5/22/2024. I got to see him talk to
Jesus before he died, and I know that he is with him in heaven.

Table of Contents

Psalm 103:20 says, "Bless the Lord, you his Angels, who excel in strength, who do his word, heeding the voice of his word." This means that by reading the poetry in this book out loud, Angels will obey the word of God and heed your prayers. Expect miracles!

The word "Rhema" in Greek means an utterance or thing said. To speak the rhema word of God is to speak scripture into your life and situation. The rhema word of God works in God's time and comes to you at the right time. You were meant to be holding this book in your hands right now!

We are living in times of warfare. There are physical, emotional, intellectual, and spiritual wars in the world today. Just as soldiers in an army must be trained to use their weapons, you as a soldier in the army of God must be trained to use your weapons. Your voice in prayer is a very powerful weapon!

The rhema word of God comes at the right time. That means that you were born at the right time, and if you read this book, you will be speaking the word of God at the right time. Ester 4:14 tells us, "Yet who knows whether you have come to the kingdom for such a time as this."

Many of the poems in this book are titled by what they were written for. Some may be titled "For Protection" or "For Healing." Underneath the title are the scriptures that were quoted in the poem. I hope that these poems inspire you to find the verses in the bible and read each chapter.

Do not underestimate the power of spoken poetry. This book is called "Powerful Poetics for Prayer" for a reason! You are speaking the word of God. It is written in

Hebrews 4:12 "For the word of God is living and powerful and sharper than any two – edged sword, piercing even to the division of soul and spirit, and of joints and marrow, and is a discerner of the thoughts and intents of the heart."

Few people truly understand the power of their words. It is important how you choose to use your words. Proverbs 18:21 says, "Death and life are in the power of the tongue, and those who love it will eat its fruit."

To add to the power of these spoken prayers I recommend first repenting of your sins. Next, find people to read these poems out loud with. Then, find a place to pray. I recommend praying in a church or on holy ground (a place that is dedicated to God). Many of these poems were written and spoken at Prayer Mountain, a holy ground that was dedicated to God in the Moravian Falls of North Carolina. In the 1700s the Moravians began 24/7 intercessory prayer that lasted 100 years. This opened heavenly portals in the Moravian Falls which are still open today. The words in this book can connect you to heaven and God's heavenly host.

When we pray with the word of God, our prayers become aligned with God's will. John 1:14 says, "Now this is the confidence that we have in him, that if we ask anything according to his will, he hears us. And if we know he hears us, whatever we ask, we know that we have the petitions that we have asked of him."

Praying with the word of God makes our prayers focused, powerful and effective. The word of God can transform our hearts and minds. I hope that as you read this book it transforms you, and your life.

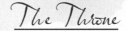

The Throne

There's a place where
grace is given freely
the impossible becomes easy
Mountains in your life are moved
And the giants you face are over – ruled.

Where snakes are chased by holy flames,
In Jesus name.
Where pain is replaced
With the promise of eternal life.
Where curses are broken,
True power awoken.
See what we can do,
Not on our own, but from the throne of God.

Gifts From Heaven

1 Corinthians 14:1, Matthew 7:7, James 1:17

I wish for Christmas gifts from heaven,
That are finer than the finest things.
I ask for the wind of the holy spirit to carry and bring
The nine spiritual gifts,
The holiest.

May they be tied to balloons and fall from the sky
Straight into God's people,
That they may prophesy.
The gift it comes down from the father of lights.
For every good gift and every perfect gift is from above.

My Christmas wish is for the gifts that only God can give.
To glorify you, Jesus our King,
This Christmas I ask for, Lord,
The word of wisdom,
The word of knowledge,
The discerning of spirits,
And especially that I may prophesy.
Ask, and it will be given to you for everyone who asks receives.

Lord, I ask for even more,
I ask for divers kinds of tongues.
I ask for the gift of faith
So that I may be saved.
I ask for the gift of healing.
And for the working of miracles
So that I may contradict natural laws
To show the world the maker of it all.

Lord, you deserve the glory!

My Christmas wish is for the gifts that only God can give.
Lord thank you for your gifts from heaven.

The North Star

John 1:4, John 3:16

On Christmas a light entered the world and defeated darkness.
The north star was born,
And God came to Earth in human form.
In him was life, and that life was the light of all people.

All constellations and creation recognized the new light in the sky,
Given to them as a sign from the creator of the universe,
That his son was born.

The star shone bright above our savior, who was a baby in a manger.
Jesus is not from Earth but from above.
We cannot know real love without knowing him.

For God so loved the world that he gave his only begotten son,
That whosoever believeth in him should not perish,
But have everlasting life.

The Shaking
Psalm 91: 11-12

There's cracks that cause shaking as we
walk along,
We can only hope that what we're standing
on is something strong.
Lord be our foundation,
We've rebuilt with every stone.
But the shaking reminds us,
Where we've been,
The grace we've been given,
And a little bit about our past.
It's time to move fast to be at our destinies
Let's keep on the path ahead.

For he shall give his angels charge over you,
To keep you in all your ways
In their hands they shall bear you up,
Lest you dash your foot against a stone.

A Prayer for the Fullness of God

Jeremiah 29: 13-14, Ephesians 3:16 - 19

My life journey is to search for and find you, God.

"You will seek me and find me when you seek me with all your heart, I will be found by you" declares the Lord.

God may your spirit strengthen my inner man with might, that Christ may dwell in my heart through faith.

May I be rooted and grounded in love, so that I can comprehend, with all the saints,

What is the width and depth and height, to know the love of Christ which passes knowledge,

That I may be filled with the fullness of God.

I was searching for you far and wide, through and deep, and I found you in me.

6

For the Renewing of Your Mind

Romans 12:2, Deuteronomy 11:19, Philippians
4:8, Colossians 3:2, Deuteronomy 11 :11

A thought can be a road,
which one will you take?
Thoughts can lead you closer to heaven or hell,
don't drive aimlessly.
Bring the map of God's word to guide you.

God do not let me be conformed to this world but transformed
through the renewing of my mind.

God help me go in the right direction, may I turn from deception
And may I never take the highway of hate.

Close the roads of lust and greed,
may I choose generosity
which leads to a land flowing with milk and honey.

I know virtue will bring me closer to you, Jesus I trust that you are
with me on this journey.
May the thoughts I choose be thoughts that are true, honest and just.
Help me think of whatsoever things are pure, lovely, and of good report.

Angels help me sort through the distractions of this world to set my
mind on things above,
and not on earthly things.

For one thought leads to another.
One road leads to another,
and the land I am crossing over to possess
is a land of hills and valleys
which drinks water from the rain of heaven.

The Promise of Glory

Romans 8:18, Galatians 2:20, Genesis 50:20, 1 Peter 4:14

God,

You were with me in my suffering when I was crucified with Christ, and I consider that the suffering that was in my life is not worth comparing to the glory that

is to be revealed in me, a daughter of the risen King.

Since I was born, I was destined to transform through your spirit.

I was created for this and made in your image.

And I believe that the evil that rose against me,

You meant for good.

To save many people alive.

Blessed am I, for glory, the spirit of God, rests upon me.

I cry out to you Lord.

You have my tongue, heart, eyes, hands, feet and innermost being.

All of me is for your glory.

Change me, I am ready to be a new creation.

It is no longer I who live but Christ who lives in me.

Like A Tree

Psalm 1:3

I shall be like a tree,
Planted by the rivers of water,
That bring forth it's fruit in its season,
Whose leaf also shall not wither;
And whatever I do shall prosper.

As the tree of my soul stands
I'll raise my hands in praise so you can see
My energy and leaves that come forth from me.
As my roots thirst for the waters of your holy spirit,
Nourishing.
Protect me that I may grow
My eyes are up to the sky as your wind and breath,
It feels like life.
You're in heaven, you're in me.
Eternal Amor, Eternal Light, Eternal Life.

Daughters of the Dawn

Jeremiah 29:11, Psalm 118:24, Isaiah 60: 3

God, I thank you for the mornings,
for the birds that sing their songs
They rejoice before we awake because they know the plans that God has made:
Plans to prosper us and not to harm us,
Plans to give us hope and a future.
And as the sun reaches the mountain peaks, may God's peace break over me.
This is a day that the Lord has made; we will rejoice and be glad in it.
And as the light shines through the clouds,
The Lord shall arise and be seen, gloriously, in thee.
Holy spirit, graciously take each morning prayer, mixed with blessings,
Poured over with promise.
God calls upon the daughters of the dawn to put into motion his plans today,
And every day, here after.

Nations will come to your light,
And kings to the brightness of your dawn.

For Restoration and Provision

Psalm 23, Psalm 46:10

Make me rest in green pastures.
Lord, you are my shepherd.
Lead me beside the still waters of your spirit,
so that I may be still and know that you are God.
Restoreth my soul,
Only you know the remedy to what ails me.
Make my body, mind, and soul new in you.
May I walk in paths of righteousness but even if I walk through the valley of
the shadow of death
I will fear no evil.
For you are with me.
The one, the son who is in me is greater than
He who is in the world.
Goodness and mercy shall follow me all the days of my life.

For Healing

Hebrews 9:14, Isaiah 53:5

The perfect prince of peace
My risen King and majesty
The lamb that died for me
His blood washes me clean of sins and iniquities.
On the cross he took on suffering and pain,
He overcame
so that we are freed by his name.
Through the eternal spirit
he offered himself without
spot to God.

His body was given up,
I drink from this cup in remembrance of him and the resurrection.
The holy spirit is bringing me life.
By his body my soul is made whole.
By his wounds I am healed.

For Protection
Psalm 91

I stand, and I am not alone.
I lift my hand and so does the Lord who is my refuge.
I abide under the shadow of the Almighty.

Though I'm small,
When I lift my arms, so does he
And his feathers are big enough to cover us all.
We shall make the Lord most high our dwelling place.
No evil shall harm us.

Lord you are my fortress.
We will not be afraid of the terror by night,
Nor of the destruction that lays waste at noonday.
We say, Father God may your angels have charge over us and guard us,
In their hands we shall be lifted up.

Lord we love you.
You are our God in whom we trust.
So let us trample serpents under our feet.
Answer us when we speak to you in prayer.
Be there in times of trouble.

Deliver us from snares and sickness and grief.
We receive long life and honor.
We believe the Lord is our salvation.

The Thousand Blessing

Deuteronomy 1:11

May The Lord God of your fathers make you a thousand times more numerous
than you are,
And bless you as he has promised you.
The beauty of your soul is unsurpassed,
and just as one flower becomes a field of one thousand,
May heaven never be out of reach.
May people seek God's presence that's wherever you are.
May God's glorious fire be in all of your pursuits
As kingdom plans are carried out through you.
May you have a thousand times more and live abundantly
In a harvest of souls.

Do everything in Love

1 Corinthians 16:14

May They Always be More
Psalm 56:8

God keeps track of all your sorrows.
He has collected all your tears in a bottle.
Your tears are counted,
From your first to your last
From the present and the past.
Like rain falling from a cloud,
God hears their sounds and knows from which they came.
Each are counted and named.
May you always have more tears from divine grace and miracles
From a father's love, as the father loves us.
From joy and blessings
From knowing how precious and cared for you are to our Lord.
May these tears always be more than those from sorrow or pain,
Heartbreak or losses,
Bad news or poor health.
May the good tears fall like rain and may you always be moved more by our
Almighty Lord.
Than by any darkness that fogs the works of God.
I hope your tears pour to water your spirit,
And bring everlasting life.

Where you go
I will go
Where you stay
I will stay

Ruth 1:16-17

The Sun and The Moon

Psalm 72:5 -7, Psalm 121:6, Jermiah 31:35

He who appoints the sun to shine by day,
Who decrees the moon and stars to shine by night,
The Lord Almighty is his name.

His name shall endure forever;
His name shall continue as long as the sun shine
Jesus, I lift you high.
For all my life I'll pray to you, I'll praise you.
During the day and night.
In his days the righteous shall flourish,
And abundance of peace,
Until the moon is no more.

The sun shall not strike me by day,
Nor the moon by night.
The Lord shall preserve my going out and my coming in.
From this time forth, forevermore.

Trust

Romans 8:38 – 39

I know that I can rest,
You have made the plans and guided my steps.
I know the time will come for revelation,
but for now I trust, you are the one true God.
The one who holds my whole heart.
I know that neither death, nor life, nor angels, nor principalities,
Nor powers, nor things present, nor things to come,
Nor height, nor depth, nor any other creature,
Shall be able to separate me from the love of God,
Which is in Christ Jesus our Lord.

Against Enemies
Psalm 35

Maybe you can't see the God watching over me.
Just below the clouds is an army far greater than anything you've
ever seen,
And he calls us Kings and Queens.
May your divine blood flow through me and bring dishonor to those
who seek my life,
Which belongs to you.
Confuse those who plot my hurt.
May an angel of the Lord pursue them.
May destruction come to them unexpectedly.
He calls us Kings and Queens

Plead my cause, O Lord
With those who strive with me; fight with those who fight against me.
Stop my enemies.

In my adversity they rejoice,
They do not speak peace,
But devise deceit
Let them not rejoice over me,
Who hate me without cause.

Awake and vindicate me!
God to you belongs all glory!
We magnify God who rescues me!
Who has pleasure in the prosperity of his servant.
We praise you all the day long!

Miracles in Time

Lamentations 3:22-23, Ecclesiastes 3:11, Psalm 31: 15,
Ephesians 5: 15-17

God I ask to step into the eternity you set inside my heart.
That it's beat and every motion in me is in sync
With the King of the Universe.

May I have understanding of the times and be wise,
Redeeming the time,
Because the days are evil.

God, I know to you a thousand years is like a day,
And you are the architect of time.
You have angels that can work through your design of time.
I need them by my side!
Jesus send them to,

Share these miracles outside, above and through,
Time with you.

Now to him who is able to do exceedingly abundantly
Above all that we ask or think
According to the power that works in us.

So if I must ask the sun to stand still, I know it will!
Because Joshua said:
"Sun, stand still over Gibeon
And moon in the valley."
So the sun stood still and the moon stopped.

God you can stop, slow down or speed up,
All the moments of our lives.
In any place, in any time,
God I ask to step into the eternity you set inside my heart.

May I share these miracles in time with you.
May we stop tragedies,
According to the multitude of your tender mercies.

Lord, may your Angels and I, go back in time.
To every moment I was defeated.
My times are in your hands.
Deliver me from the hands of my enemies,
From those who pursue me.
Lord, you deserve the glory!

Lord, thank you for your favor and salvation.
The steadfast love of the Lord never ceases,
his mercies never come to an end; they are new
every morning.

Standing Against Giants

1 Samuel 17:32, 1 Samuel 17:45,

The bigger the enemy the bigger the victory
As hostility is in the air we breathe
And they are angry that we're alive.
For the war is over our souls
And I won't let darkness take hold.

Let no one lose heart on account of these giants,
God's servants will go fight them.

In the second of life and death just take a step of faith
And answer me,
Do you think they're bigger than God?
Because I assure you they're not.
The bigger the enemy the bigger the victory.

In this second of time, all of your pain, all of your fear,
Do you think it's bigger than God?
Because I can assure you
Everything you are,
Is everything they're not!
Don't let this city fall.
Just know that God is bigger than it all.

You come against us with weapons made of the Earth
But we come against you in the name of the Lord of hosts,
The God of the armies of Israel, whom you have defied.

Why Are You Afraid?

Psalm 27:1, Psalm 46

If love wrote your destiny
And brought you each step of the way.
If love made you brave,
And grace was enough to save your life,
Why wouldn't you trust in God's plan for you?
The one who made your soul,
Created and formed you as a babe.
Maybe, what's in you,
Is bigger than you.
And you're linked to the stars, eternity, and everything.
When you breathe and when your heart beats,
Believe that what you were made to be
Is bigger than your situation,
This nation,
And any of your enemies.

Tell me,
Why are you afraid?

The Lord is my light and my salvation; whom shall I fear?
The Lord is the strength of my life;
Of whom shall I be afraid?

God is in the midst of her, she shall not be moved.
For the Lord of hosts is with us.

Against The Spirit of Death

Psalm 118 – 17, 1 Corinthians 15:54, Psalm 49:15, Psalm 9:13, Hebrews 2:9,
Psalm 86:2, Psalm 86:16

God, my father,
You fashioned me in my mother's womb,
You chose the day that I was born and sent angels into the room.
You also chose the day that I would die,
And I know it's not my appointed time.

God will redeem my soul from the power of the grave,
For he shall receive me.
Have mercy on me, O Lord!
You who lifts me up from the gates of death.

There will be no early weeping, no early tears, my life will have an abundance
of years.
Through Jesus's suffering of death, he is crowned with glory and honor, that
he, by the grace of God,
has tasted death for everyone.

I shall not die, but live, and declare the works of the Lord!
God, you hold my heart may you embark on each journey with me.
God I ask that you put angels on task to make my life last,
as I fulfill your will.
I heed heaven to hear this petitioned prayer.

Preserve my life, give your strength to your servant.

I decree, death is swallowed up in victory!

Today Is Not My Last

Psalm 30: 2-5

I will be lifted up from my despair with an answered prayer.
You hear my cries and you're healing me,
You're saving my life!
God you brought my soul up from the grave,
You have kept me alive.

Today is not my last.
Praise the Messiah, who died.
In his name I arise, sing, and rejoice!
Because the Lord brings glory and gladness.

38

The Abrahamic Blessing

Genesis 12: 1-3

For the flag I should take up?
May it have a lion and a crown.
For I know my kingdom is eternal
But countries rise and fall like a wave of sound.

You drew a family tree diagram,
But if you looked into my father's garden, you'd see the tree of life.
He made paradise.
I'm a son of God.

He made us different in our customs and in the way we look or sound
But brother, we're from the kingdom.
We are sons of God.

Live a life of obedience to God and seek him in prayer.
May he show you the land he has for you and take you there.

For God has said:
"I will make you a great nation;
I will bless you
And make your name great;
And you shall be a blessing.
I will bless those who bless you,
And I will curse him who curses you;
And in you all the families of the Earth shall be blessed."

 The Home Blessing

John 14:23, Psalm 16:8, Exodus 33:14-16, Psalm 16:11, Revelation 3:20

"If anyone loves me, he will keep my word and my father will love him and make a home with him."
Holy spirit come into my home.
Fill every room, shine through every window.
May God's presence be on each step, may I keep the Lord always before me,
Even when I dream.
Before I go to sleep, may God's presence go with me and give me rest.
God Bless this Home.

Jesus you are the great priest over this place, use this space for miracles.
Lord I dedicate this home to you.

Holy spirit dwell in my living room
"For in God's presence there is fullness of joy."
God deploy angels of joy and peace to each gathering here.
As we draw near to God may he draw near to us.

Jesus as I sit down to eat, may I hear your voice.
"Behold I stand at the door and knock. If anyone hears my voice and opens the door, then I will come dine with him, and him with me."
May this home be an earthly headquarters for God's Kingdom.

Holy spirit come into my home.
Fill every room, shine through every window.

For Refuge
Psalm 18

My mind, my strength and sanctified soul is not enough for this battle.
God have favor on me and be my savior.
May you arrive on the wings of the wind.
Make darkness your canopy,
Gather the waters, and thick clouds of the skies
May brightness shine and coals of fire flame forth before you.
May the utterance of your voice send out arrows to scatter my enemies,
lightning to confuse and trouble them.
God take me away keep me safe.

Friend who reads the words from this pen:
Keep the ways of the Lord.
Stay free of guilt and iniquity.
I pray that God will save you,
Shall you ever need refuge.

The Double Blessing

Isaiah 61: 1-9

I am a priest of the Lord.
I am a servant of our God.
I'll find my flock
And protect them from what lurks in the shadows.

I'll serve as Jesus did.
I won't forget to forgive.
Instead of shame I shall have double honor.
And instead of confusion I shall rejoice in my portion.

Therefore, in my land I shall possess double,
Everlasting joy shall be mine.

Eyes to See and Ears to Hear

Matthew 13: 16-17, Psalm 143:8

Whether it be a white feather, a butterfly, or a ray of golden light,
God is always sending signs that heaven has transcended into our lives.
God open the eyes of my heart
Whether it be through wisdom, revelation or contemplation of your everlasting
love for me,
May I have eyes to see and ears to hear.

Let me hear in the morning of your steadfast love,
For in you I trust.
Make me know the way I should go,
for to you I lift up my soul.

A Glory Cover

Habakkuk 2:12

"For the Earth will be filled with the Knowledge of the glory of the Lord as the
waters cover the sea."
It is my destiny to carry this lamp
To breathe more than air
To see more than what's physically there.
To be everything he's called me to be.
To bring miracles
And to speak in heavenly realms.

I know what comes from the throne of God is beyond Earth.
May his glory cover me as the waters cover the sea.

A Prayer to Usher in America's Golden Age

Luke 3:17, Ephesians 5:11-14, Galatians 5:13, John 8:32,
2 Corinthians 3:18, Isaiah 9:6-7, Malachi 3:2

We've been baptized with fire and shine brighter in the dark.
Can you see us?
The red, white and blue flames
Turning and burning,
Purifying this land.

God by your hand,
Separate the wheat from the chaff
What brings us life and what brings us death
Incinerate the plans of the wicked.
We've been set apart to bring light to the dark.
May we take no part in the works of darkness but instead expose them.
For what is manifest by the light is made visible.

We are called to liberty
May the truth set us free.

From glory to glory,
America's government rests on our savior's shoulders.
Holy spirit set us ablaze to be red, white and blue flames.
God with your refiner's fire,
make America pure gold.

For the Outnumbered
Psalm 3

I will not be afraid of ten thousand people.
I will stay still,
I will wait.
I will patiently know,
His spirit in me can overthrow any enemy.

I'll send silent battle cries in prayer.
I'll peacefully proclaim my salvation belongs to the Lord.
You are a shield for me, my glory.
Thou they be many,
Against one, with God's son.

I will not be afraid of ten thousand people!

For Angelic Aide

Daniel 7: 21 – 22, Psalm 70:1

I need to speak in tongues,
I need to call upon the eternal Kingdom.
That sits high above the Earth.
Seraphim, Cherubin, warrior angels, messenger angels,
I need every single one.

Make haste, O God, to deliver me;
Make haste to help me, O Lord.

Angels, mix what I say with the intent of heaven,
To help me pray.

And God, if what you see makes you angry have your angels
pour out your wrath on all who are after me.

And the four winds, God speed any wind
You think I need.
And may the prince Saint Michael,
lead his army into war for me.

For the Ancient of Days made a judgement in favor of the saints of the Most High
And the time has come for the saints to possess the kingdom.

Printed in the United States
by Baker & Taylor Publisher Services